Y is for Yorick

For Nate,
my favorite prince of Denmark

Y is for Yorick

**A Slightly Irreverent
Shakespearean ABC Book
for Grown-Ups**

By Jennifer Adams

Illustrations by Hugh D'Andrade

GIBBS SMITH

TO ENRICH AND INSPIRE HUMANKIND

First Edition
15 14 13 12 11   5 4 3 2 1

Published by
Gibbs Smith
P.O. Box 667
Layton, Utah 84041

1.800.835.4993 orders
www.gibbs-smith.com
www.wordmusings.com

Designed by Ron Stucki
Printed and bound in China

Gibbs Smith books are printed on either recycled, 100% post-consumer
waste, FSC-certified papers or on paper produced from sustainable PEFC-
certified forest/controlled wood source. Learn more at www.pefc.org.

Library of Congress Cataloging-in-Publication Data
Adams, Jennifer.
Y is for Yorick : a slightly irreverent Shakespearean ABC book for
grown-ups / Jennifer Adams ; illustrations by Hugh D'Andrade.—1st ed.
     p. cm.

ISBN 978-1-4236-0754-0
1. Shakespeare, William, 1564-1616—Dictionaries. 2. Shakespeare,
William, 1564-1616—Humor. 3. Characters and characteristics in
literature—Dictionaries. I. Title.
PR2892.A37 2011
822.3'3—dc22
                              2010037775

Contents

*Thanks to
Lisa Anderson, my skilled
and incredibly patient editor;
Ron Stucki, my lovely and
brilliant designer;
and Hugh D'Andrade, for
amazing illustrations.*

Why Shakespeare Still Reigns

In 1592, Shakespeare was called by contemporary Robert Greene an "upstart crow." Voltaire called the play *Hamlet* "a crude and barbarous piece, which the lowest rabble in France and Italy would not stand for" and the product of "the imagination of a drunken savage." Yet with these notable exceptions, we are hard-pressed to find anyone who does not consider Shakespeare a genius. (Besides, keep in mind that Voltaire was French!) In fact, Shakespeare is fairly universally acknowledged as the greatest writer who ever lived. His plays have been translated into every major language and are performed more often than those of any other playwright. For more than four hundred years, the best writers and thinkers of the world tend to side with Sir Laurence Oliver, who said of Shakespeare that he is "the nearest thing in incarnation to the eye of God."

William Shakespeare was born in 1564, lived in London and Stratford, and died at the age of fifty-two. He wrote thirty-seven plays, 164 sonnets, and several long poems. Unlike many of the greatest writers, he was successful in his own lifetime. The Bard was a working writer and actor who understood the balance between art and finance, a question artists and producers still struggle with to this day. Shakespeare's work appealed to the masses as well as the elite: his plays were meant to be enjoyed by both prostitutes and the queen. He wrote with brilliance, depth, humor, clarity, and humanity.

Shakespeare borrowed plots and story lines, and his work is indeed the best example of plagiarism that is so elevated by the borrower that it becomes much more celebrated and memorable than the original. Many of his story lines were taken from earlier sources. He borrowed from history and from the writing of Petrarch. *King Lear* is based on the story of King Leir in *Historia Regum Britanniae* by Geoffrey of Monmouth. One of Prospero's speeches in *The Tempest* is taken word for word from a speech by Medea in Ovid's poem Metamorphoses. Shakespeare's retellings influence how we remember history as well. For example, we think of Macbeth as a murderer who was disastrous as a king, when actual history suggests Macbeth was a fair and able ruler. And history says Richard III had no physical deformities, but because of Shakespeare we remember him as a hunchback.

The plays of Shakespeare have become ingrained in us as part of our cultural identity. Who does not think of Romeo and Juliet as the greatest tragic lovers of all time? Doesn't think of "Et tu, Brute?" as the line of true betrayal? Doesn't see Hamlet as the ultimate contemplator of our existence in his speech: "To be or not to be, that is the question."

Characters such as Hamlet, Othello, Ophelia, Richard III, Shylock, Puck, and Falstaff have entered our consciousness and taken up residence there.

Additionally, famous lines from Shakespeare abound in our daily vernacular: "To thine own self be true," "Beware the Ides of March," "What fools these mortals be," "Would a rose by any other name smell as sweet?" "Nothing can come of nothing," "A horse, a horse, my kingdom for a horse!" "There is method to the madness," "All that glistens is not gold," "Brave new world,"

"Parting is such sweet sorrow," "We are such stuff as dreams are made on," and "He was a man of infinite jest" are quotations we use and hear perhaps without even realizing where they come from.

Shakespeare can be bawdy, risqué, and downright funny. Those who become overwhelmed by the Elizabethan English, or don't stop to listen to what he is actually saying, might be shocked at all the jokes they are missing about farting, all the insults, all the blatant sexual talk. "Pillicock" and "clack-dish" may pass you by if you're not listening closely, but all that talk of plowing furrows and sheathing swords should not. "Venus' glove" is a fairly obvious reference; "a three-inch fool" quite the insult! And it's hard to imagine he's referring to anything but sex in the injunctions to "hang one's bugle in an invisible baldric" or "make the beast with two backs."

Shakespeare can also be romantically sublime. From *Romeo and Juliet* alone we read, "But, soft! what light through yonder window breaks? It is the east, and Juliet is the sun. Arise, fair sun, and kill the envious moon, who is already sick and pale with grief, that thou her maid art far more fair than she." And "My bounty is as boundless as the sea, my love as deep; the more I give to thee, the more I have, for both are infinite." And "It was the lark, the herald of the morn, no nightingale: look, love, what envious streaks do lace the severing clouds in yonder east: Night's candles are burnt out, and jocund day stands tiptoe on the misty mountain tops." Can anything more beautiful have ever been written?

And Shakespeare makes us think. A brilliant portrayal of *The Merchant of Venice*, written almost four hundred years before the Holocaust, says more about Jews and Christians and how they interact and how a society can create people that behave in abhorrent ways and what is justice and what is mercy than perhaps anything written since—all questions still relevant, all questions that have not and probably never will be satisfactorily answered, but all questions a society must examine. *Othello* teaches us about jealousy and rage and murder. All with a complex overlayering of questions about interracial marriage. *King Lear* shows the tragic result of stubbornness and pride, and what greed does to some, and the complexities of relationships between aging parents and their children. Shakespeare tackles the hardest themes: loyalty, prejudice, jealousy, revenge, pride, ambition, and war. Justice and mercy, love and hate, sex and death. Shakespeare is such a great writer in part because he is so contemporary—his themes at once universal, modern, and timeless.

And then in the end it is the language! All these things presented in language you could listen to forever. The poetry and grandeur of it. Language like music, layered with so much meaning you could never unravel it completely.

Shakespeare is a prism into which we put our own questions, prejudices, ideas, and ideologies and out come a million different interpretations that make us view the world each time in a new light, in a new way. He makes us ask the hard questions, then makes us look deep within ourselves for answers.

As a playwright, a poet, a wordsmith, Shakespeare still reigns. There is no one who compares.

ABCs

  is for Ariel.

Ariel was a **graceful, efficient, good** servant whose acts led people toward better lives. Of course, Ariel was a fairy and was **not real**.

 is for
Beatrice and
Benedick.

Beatrice and Benedick were a **couple** of Italians who were **constantly fighting** and insulting each other. Eventually they decided **they were in love.**

B is also for Bottom.

Bottom was a self-important, working-class man that, like many people, went around among friends and colleagues not realizing he was an ass.

 is for Cleopatra.

Cleopatra was a **beautiful** and histrionic queen who **lost her lover** as well as her political power and **killed herself** with a poisonous snake. Cleopatra cornered the market on **drama queen** for all time.

Antony and Cleopatra

 **is also for Claudius.**

He **killed his brother** and **married** his **brother's widow**, Gertrude. However, he **forgot** to take into account **the stepchildren.**

Hamlet

D is for Desdemona.

Desdemona was a **virtuous** and **beautiful** woman. Many **people admire her** for choosing her own husband rather than letting her father arrange the marriage. Unfortunately it **did not turn out too well** for her in the end.

Othello

D is also for Dennis.

Dennis was a **very minor** character who **no one remembers.**

  is for Edmund.

Edmund was a **bastard**.

King Lear

 is for Falstaff.

Falstaff was the **portly friend** of Prince Hal. He teaches us that you can be **a drunk, thief, liar,** and **coward** and still be **loved** if you can make people laugh.

G is for Ghost.

Banquo, Julius Caesar, and
Old Hamlet all made **excellent ghosts.**

Macbeth
Julius Caesar
Hamlet

H is for Hamlet.

Hamlet was a young man who **had a hard time making decisions.**
He was also a prince. Young people should not be like Hamlet, who was **responsible for the deaths** of his fiancé, future father-in-law, brother-in-law, stepfather, and mother, all because he had a lot of **trouble with follow-through.**

Hamlet

H is also for Henry V.

Henry was a **nice young man** who made **inspiring** speeches and **conquered France.**

Henry V

 **is additionally for Henry VIII.**

Henry the VIII was a **fat and licentious** king. He **liked to divorce** his wives or sometimes **cut their heads off**. He was the first of what we today would call a **serial monogamist**.

Henry VIII

i is for Iago.

Iago was a **malevolent guy** who **destroyed** the life of **his boss** simply because he could. If he were around today he **would probably be a lawyer.**

Othello

 is for Juliet.

Juliet teaches all young girls that **if you truly love** someone, wholly and completely, it **will be the death of you.**

Romeo and Juliet

 is also
for Julius Caesar.

Julius Caesar was the most **important** **leader** in the history of Rome. But he was **not very good at choosing friends.**

Julius Caesar

 **is for Katharine of Aragon.**

Katharine was the **first wife** of Henry VIII and had the misfortune of not producing a male heir. She was also **Spanish** and **overly religious,** both of which **seemed to annoy** Henry.

Henry VIII

L is for Lear.

Lear was a **king** who had a
serious problem with estate management.
He is a **good example** of why
you should not let your family
read your will until **after you're dead.**

King Lear

  is for Macbeth.

Macbeth was someone who was **bullied by his wife**'s ambitions, and it got him a job he couldn't handle. He **shouldn't have listened** to the **witches** either.

Macbeth

 **is for Nurse.**

The Nurse was Juliet's surrogate mother and confidante. Everyone wishes they had someone in their life like the Nurse.

 is for Ophelia.

Ophelia was a young woman who **spent too much time letting other people tell her what to do** rather than thinking for herself. Young women should not be like Ophelia, or **instead of being the Queen** of Denmark they will **end up drowned** in some river or another.

Hamlet

is also
for Othello.

Othello was a **successful general** who got some bad information. He also had a **problem with jealousy.** Othello was like the **original O. J.** Simpson, except he **did not get away with it.**

Othello

 **is for Polonius.**

Polonius was a **long-winded blowhard** who was always giving unwanted advice. Eventually **Hamlet killed him**.

Hamlet

P is also for Prospero.

Prospero was a bit of a **control freak** who **liked the special effects.** But who knows what any of us would do with **unlimited time** on a deserted island and a **book of magical spells?**

The Tempest

 is additionally for Puck.

Puck was like Cupid, except he tended to make the wrong people fall in love with each other.

A Midsummer Night's Dream

 is for Queen,

the **wife of Cymbeline**, King of Britain. She was one of the **original evil stepmothers**.

  is for Romeo.

Romeo was **one of the greatest romantic lovers** of all time. He is also a good example of why it is important to **get along with your in-laws** if you want your marriage to last.

Romeo and Juliet

R is also for Richard III.

Richard was a **treacherous hunchback** who **murdered** his two young nephews in order **to become king.** He also had the **bad manners** to propose marriage to the Lady Anne on the way to her husband's **funeral.**

Richard III

R is additionally for Rosencrantz.

Rosencrantz and Guildenstern

are dead.

Hamlet

 **is for Shylock.**

Shylock was **a loan shark** who got a **bad rap** for being **Jewish.** He also had a **problem knowing when** it was time to let something drop.

 is for Titus Andronicus.

Titus was a fairly **brutal Roman general** bent on revenge. He **wasn't very popular**, and still isn't.

Titus Andronicus

 is for Ursula.

Ursula was a **maid** who **nobody remembers** either. If you want to be remembered it is **better to be** a queen, king, murderer, cross-dresser, or ghost.

is for Viola.

Viola was a **girl** who **dressed up as a boy**, who **fell in love with a man** (who thought she was a boy). Another woman fell in love with Viola, but ended up marrying her twin brother (who really was a boy). Today we would say Viola had some serious **transgender identity issues**.

Twelfth Night

W is for Witches.

The Three Witches who showed up on the moors caused all sorts of trouble. But people tend to forgive them because they repeat this catchy line: "Double, double toil and trouble; fire burn, and cauldron bubble."

Macbeth

  is for PoliXenes.

Polixenes was the **King of Bohemia.**
He spent about **sixteen years fleeing**
from some people and **chasing** others.
These shenanigans eventually **culminated**
at a **sheep-shearing** festival.

The Winter's Tale

is for Yorick.

He was **a man**
of infinite jest.

Hamlet

Z is for Elizabeth.

She was the **wife of Edward IV** and **involved with Richard III**. But the relationships with these kings and queens are so convoluted **not even Shakespeare** can **make sense** of them.

Richard III

Play
Summaries

Antony and Cleopatra

Mark Antony and Cleopatra are madly in love. Antony is one of the three rulers of Rome's triumvirate, along with Lepidus and Octavius Caesar, but spends his time in Egypt where he conducts a very public affair with Cleopatra. Cleopatra is the queen of Egypt. She is beautiful, sexual, and highly dramatic. A message arrives that Antony's wife is dead and that Pompey is raising an army to overthrow the triumvirate. Against Cleopatra's wishes, Antony returns to Rome.

In Rome, Antony has a fight with Caesar. In order to heal the relationship, he agrees to marry Caesar's sister Octavia. When Cleopatra learns that Antony has married Octavia she flies into a jealous rage; she is only appeased when she is told Octavia is ugly.

The triumvirate meets with Pompey and they come to a truce without going to battle. That evening the four men drink together to celebrate their alliance. One of Pompey's soldiers suggests a plan to assassinate the triumvirate, but Pompey refuses.

Antony leaves Rome for Athens, and Caesar breaks the newly formed truce and attacks Pompey. He uses Lepidus's army to help him to victory, then turns on Lepidus and accuses him of treason. When Antony learns of the betrayal, he is incensed with Caesar. Antony sends Octavia off to Rome and returns to Egypt and Cleopatra. In Egypt, he raises a large army to come against Caesar. Caesar is furious at Antony's treatment of his sister and raises an army as well.

Antony agrees to fight at sea and allows Cleopatra to command a ship. In the heat of the battle, she flees and Antony loses. He condemns Cleopatra, but almost immediately forgives her.

Meanwhile, Caesar sends a messenger to Cleopatra to convince her to betray Antony to him. She is actually entertaining this idea when Antony discovers the plot. He accuses her of treachery, but only moments later, forgives her. At this point, his loyal friend Enobarbus deserts Antony and joins Caesar's camp. When Antony learns of Enobarbus's desertion, he feels responsibility rather than anger and sends his friend's possessions to him. Enobarbus is so overcome by this gesture that he dies of a broken heart.

Antony and Cleopatra again meet Caesar's forces in battle at sea. And, yet again, Cleopatra flees with her ship at the crucial moment, allowing Antony's defeat. This time it is too much. Antony vows to kill Cleopatra; she sequesters herself in her family's tomb and sends word that she has committed suicide. When he hears Cleopatra is dead, Antony is grief-torn and vows to kill himself. He falls on his sword, but does not die immediately. He is carried to Cleopatra in her tomb and dies in her arms.

Caesar takes Cleopatra prisoner. Rather than suffer the humiliation of being shown as a prize of victory in the streets of Rome, she kills herself with a poisonous asp.

As You Like It

$\mathcal{D}$uke Frederick has usurped the throne of Duke Senior, and Duke Senior has fled to the forest of Ardenne, where he lives with a band of followers. Frederick allows Senior's daughter, Rosalind, to remain at court because she is the best friend of his own daughter, Celia.

Meanwhile, Sir Rowland has died and left all his wealth to his eldest son, Oliver, with the understanding that Oliver is to take care of his brother Orlando. But Oliver is greedy and resents Orlando—he denies him wealth, position, or training.

When Orlando comes to court and beats the court wrestler in a fight, Orlando and Rosalind fall instantly in love. Orlando returns home and learns that Oliver is now plotting to kill him. He flees to the forest of Ardenne.

Duke Frederick decides to banish Rosalind from court. She escapes to the safety of Ardenne Forest, taking Celia with her. For protection, Rosalind dresses as a man and calls herself Ganymede, and Celia dresses as a shepherdess and calls herself Aliena.

Duke Frederick is furious when he discovers his daughter, Celia, is gone. He orders Oliver to lead a manhunt against Orlando and decides to raise an army against his own brother, Duke Senior.

Meanwhile, in the forest, Orlando comes upon Duke Senior's camp and is accepted into his company. When Rosalind and Celia arrive, they soon meet a lovesick young shepherd named Silvius. He is hopelessly infatuated with Phoebe, who scorns him.

Rosalind, still disguised as the young man Ganymede, soon crosses paths with Orlando. He is as lovesick as Silvius, pining away for Rosalind. Ganymede tells Orlando that she can cure him of his lovesickness if he will meet with her every day, pretend she is Rosalind, and proclaim his love to her. Orlando agrees.

Phoebe, who is increasingly cruel in her rejection of Silvius, meets Rosalind, who is still dressed as Ganymede. Thinking her to be a young man, she falls in love with him.

One day Orlando doesn't show up for his love lessons. Rosalind learns that he came upon his brother Oliver in the forest, who was being attacked by a lion. Orlando saved Oliver from certain death and the two are reconciled.

Oliver and Celia meet and fall in love and agree to marry. Phoebe keeps pursuing Ganymede, and Orlando gets tired of proclaiming his love for Rosalind to a boy. Rosalind decides it's time to end the charade.

She promises Ganymede will marry Phoebe and has everyone gather in the forest for the wedding. Rosalind then gets Phoebe to agree that if for some reason she refuses to marry Ganymede, she will marry Silvius instead. Rosalind also gets Duke Senior (her father) to agree that he would allow his daughter to marry Orlando if she were present. Rosalind and Celia leave and reenter as themselves. Rosalind marries Orlando, Celia marries Oliver, and the disgruntled Phoebe marries the delighted Silvius.

During the nuptial celebrations news arrives that on his way to attack them, Duke Frederick met a holy man who convinced him to give up his violent ways and become a monk. Duke Senior and all the company are therefore free to return to court.

Cymbeline

The Queen, wife of King Cymbeline, desires the ascension of her son Cloten to the British throne. She wants the Princess Imogen, daughter of Cymbeline by his first wife, to marry her son. But Imogen is in love with the lowly born Posthumus. Imogen marries Posthumus in secret. When they are discovered, Cymbeline imprisons Imogen and banishes Posthumus to Italy.

In Italy, Posthumus meets the clever and manipulative Iachimo. Iachimo convinces him that all women are unfaithful and as proof says he can seduce Imogen. He travels to the British court and attempts to do so. His attempts fail, as have the continued attempts of Cloten to seduce the princess. But Iachimo does not give up so easily. He hides himself in a trunk that is placed in Imogen's bedchamber. Once she is sleeping, he sneaks out and watches her, takes note of the details of her room, and steals her bracelet. He then returns to Posthumus with the bracelet and details of Imogen's room. Posthumus believes that Imogen has been unfaithful to him and sends orders for his servant Pisanio to kill her.

Pisanio, however, believes Imogen is innocent. He tells her to disguise herself as a boy and go in search of her banished husband.

Imogen becomes lost in the wilds of Wales. There she stumbles upon Guiderius and Arviragus. Unbeknownst to her or to them, they are her own brothers, brought up by a nobleman who was unjustly banished by Cymbeline.

Cloten pursues Imogen to Wales; he plans to kill Posthumus and rape Imogen wearing Posthumus's clothing. Instead he encounters Guiderius, whom he challenges to a fight. Guiderius kills Cloten and cuts off his head.

In the meantime, Imogen, feeling unwell, drinks a potion that she has been told is medicinal. The Queen has had the potion made as a poison. The potion doesn't kill Imogen, but induces a deep sleep.

Imogen's brothers and the nobleman find her and think she is dead; they place her body beside the slain Cloten. When Imogen awakes she finds herself next to the dead, headless body of Cloten wearing her husband's clothing. She thinks it is Posthumus and falls into despair. An invading Roman army has come to Britain, and Imogen, still disguised as a boy, hires herself out to the army as a page.

Posthumus and Iachimo are with the Roman army. Posthumus changes into the clothes of a British peasant and fights against Rome, then after Britain wins the battle, switches into Roman garb and is taken prisoner. He is wracked with grief and guilt, believing he is responsible for his wife's death, and seeks to punish himself.

The prisoners are brought before King Cymbeline and the truth is revealed: Imogen is reunited with Posthumus; Iachimo confesses his deception and is forgiven; the identity of Guiderius and Arviragus is revealed. The Queen confesses that she never loved Cymbeline and planned to poison him slowly so that her son would inherit the throne; she then dies of a fever.

Hamlet

On a frozen Danish wasteland outside the castle of Elsinore, a ghost appears. It is the old King Hamlet. The ghost tells young Hamlet, Prince of Denmark, that he (the king) was murdered by his brother Claudius (Hamlet's uncle), who poured poison in his ear while he was sleeping. Claudius took his throne and married his widow Gertrude (Hamlet's mother). The ghost asks Hamlet to avenge his murder, and Hamlet agrees.

Hamlet decides to act like he is mad, thinking erratic behavior might give him access to information and afford him an opportunity to kill his uncle.

Hamlet has been courting Ophelia and she is in love with him. Her father, Polonius, and her brother, Laertes, do not think Hamlet is serious about her and have been trying to get her to break it off. Hamlet begins behaving strangely toward Ophelia and treating her horribly. Polonius reports this behavior to Claudius and Gertrude. Claudius sends Hamlet's boyhood friends Rosencrantz and Guildenstern to spy on him.

Hamlet is torn between belief that the ghost was his father and he must avenge him and that it was some dark spirit sent to get him to commit murder. When a visiting acting troupe comes to court, he decides they should reenact the murder and he will watch his uncle's response. When the murder is performed onstage, Claudius is visibly shaken.

Gertrude summons Hamlet to her room to explain

his strange behavior. While he is there, Polonius is hiding behind the curtain eavesdropping. He makes a noise and Hamlet, thinking him to be Claudius, stabs him to death.

Fearing for his life, Claudius concocts a plan to send Hamlet on a supposed diplomatic mission to England; in reality, once he is abroad he is to be murdered. Rosencrantz and Guildenstern go with him. The plan goes awry: Hamlet escapes and sends his friends Rosencrantz and Guildenstern to their deaths instead.

Ophelia, heartbroken over Hamlet's treatment of her and the brutal death of her father, goes mad. Laertes is enraged at Hamlet because of his sister's madness and his father's death. He and Claudius make a plan. Laertes will challenge Hamlet to a fencing match. His sword tip will be poisoned and thus he can kill Hamlet by merely scratching him with it. As a backup plan, Claudius will offer Hamlet a goblet of poisoned wine. Meanwhile, Ophelia drowns herself.

Two gravediggers are digging Ophelia's grave. Hamlet arrives at the scene. One of the gravediggers unearths the skull of Yorick, the old court jester, whom Hamlet knew well. The funeral procession arrives and Hamlet and Laertes get into a fistfight over the open grave.

Laertes and Hamlet meet for the fencing match. The match begins and death ensues: Gertrude toasts Hamlet and drinks from the poisoned goblet, Laertes pierces Hamlet with the poisoned blade, Hamlet in turn cuts Laertes with the same blade. Hamlet stabs Claudius with the poisoned blade, then makes him drink from the poisoned goblet for good measure.

When Fortinbras, a neighboring prince, arrives on the scene, he finds the royal family dead. In his dying moments, Hamlet has named Fortinbras as successor to the Danish throne.

Henry V

*Y*oung Prince Hal indulged in a wild adolescence, consorting with thieves, drunkards, and prostitutes at the Boar's Head Tavern on the seedy side of London. Now his father, Henry IV, is dead, and Prince Hal must prove himself as a worthy king: Henry V.

Henry decides to lay claim to certain parts of France. The French prince sends an insulting message to Henry in response to these claims, including a gift of tennis balls to make fun of Henry's idleness and youth. Angered, Henry decides to invade France. He is supported by English noblemen, as well as the clergy, and begins to prepare for war.

At the Boar's Head Tavern, some of the men prepare to leave their families for the war. Bardolph, Pistol, and Nim are petty thieves, former friends of Henry whom he renounced when he was crowned king. Pistol and Nim are fighting over the Mistress Quickly, who promised to marry Nim but married Pistol instead. A boy comes to the tavern to announce that John Falstaff, the elderly knight who was once Prince Hal's best friend, is dying. Shortly after, Falstaff is dead.

A group of traitors are working with the French to plan Henry's death. He discovers the plot, and Scrope, one of his old friends, is involved. They beg for mercy, but Henry sentences them all to death.

In France, Henry fights his way across the country with his troops, conquering and giving inspiring speeches to motivate his soldiers to victory. With the help of the Welsh captain Fluellen, the town of Harfluer surrenders, and Henry makes it a base from which to continue his war.

Bardolph and Nim are caught looting and are sentenced to death by hanging. Henry shows no remorse for this, despite their former friendship.

The climax of the war comes at the Battle of Agincourt, where the French outnumber the English five to one. The night before the battle, Henry disguises himself as a common soldier. Wearing a dirty old cloak, he moves among the camp, learning what his men think of him. Alone, he bemoans the role of a monarch, which is full of loneliness and responsibility.

The morning comes and Henry rouses his men with a stirring St. Crispin's Day speech: "We few, we happy few, we band of brothers." The men who fight together this day, he says, will be bound together for life and will have something to speak of and remember with supreme pride from now until their old age. The men are inspired, the battle rages, and the English win the day.

Later the peace negotiations are worked out. The King of France will be allowed to keep his throne, but Henry will marry Catherine, daughter of the French king. Henry's future son will be the king of France, and thus the marriage will unite the two kingdoms.

Henry VIII

Lord Buckingham is angry. He resents Cardinal Wolsey's power and disproportionate influence over the king. Buckingham is arrested for treason on Wolsey's orders. At his hearing, Buckingham is accused of assuming he is next in line for the throne if Henry dies without a male heir. Henry is convinced of Buckingham's guilt, but Queen Katharine is not. Buckingham is sentenced to death.

In disguise, Henry attends a fancy dinner ball at Wolsey's home. There he meets Anne Bullen and falls in love with her.

On the streets, talk turns to the king's plan to divorce his wife Katharine. When Anne hears this, she feels sorry for Katharine and thinks how she would never want to be queen. Immediately afterwards, she receives a title and money from Henry as a sign of his affection.

At a trial with a cardinal from Rome in attendance, Henry argues that his marriage to Katharine is unlawful and should be dissolved. Katharine begs him to remain loyal to her—she has been an honest and faithful wife for twenty years. Katharine accuses Wolsey of his role in her undoing. She then leaves the proceedings. Later, the cardinal and Wolsey try to convince Katharine to submit to the divorce in a way that will allow her to remain under the king's care, but Katharine is outraged by the suggestion.

Wolsey, in fact, has been playing both sides in the matter of the king's divorce. He tells Henry he is working for the divorce, but secretly writes the Pope telling him to refuse to grant it. Henry intercepts this letter, which also contains proof of money and possessions Wolsey has seized from other nobles and kept for himself. When Henry confronts Wolsey, he admits his guilt.

Henry's divorce is granted. He then announces his marriage to Anne. Wolsey dies, and Katharine, who feels that she will die soon herself, forgives him.

In the meantime, Thomas Cromwell has gained the king's support at court. The king also discovers a plot against his friend Cranmer, the Archbishop of Canterbury. He gives Cranmer his ring as a sign of support. Cranmer is called before the council. After questioning, they wish to strip him of his rank and remove him to the Tower; Cranmer stops the guards by showing the king's ring. Henry himself enters and chastises the council, telling them to get along with one another.

Anne Bullen gives birth to a little girl. The English people gather in the streets for a procession to see her christened. She is named Elizabeth and is foretold to be one of England's greatest rulers.

Julius Caesar

Gaius Cassius and others are conspiring to assassinate Julius Caesar. Cassius tries to persuade Brutus, Caesar's close friend, that Caesar is getting too powerful and wants to turn Rome into a dictatorship. Later Cassius and Cinna plant forged documents incriminating Caesar to try to recruit Brutus to their cause. Brutus is reluctantly won over.

A soothsayer tells Caesar to beware the Ides of March. Caesar's wife, Calpurnia, wakes from a horrible nightmare and also tries to persuade Caesar not to attend the senate that day. Caesar goes anyway and is stabbed to death by the conspirators.

Mark Antony, Caesar's right-hand man, asks to speak at Caesar's funeral, pretending that Caesar's murderers are his friends. At the funeral, Brutus very logically explains to the citizens of Rome why they killed Caesar and gains their support. Then Mark Antony speaks. Playing on emotion, he condemns Caesar's murder and turns the crowd against Brutus, Cassius, and the others. The crowd goes after the conspirators and Brutus and Cassius flee. The mob kills an innocent poet, also named Cinna.

An army led by Mark Antony and Octavius pursues Cassius and Brutus. Cassius and Brutus argue. Brutus sees Caesar's ghost, who says he will greet him again at Philippi.

On the Plains of Philippi, Antony's and Octavius's forces face Brutus's and Cassius's forces. Through confusion in battle, Cassius thinks Brutus's forces have been captured, so he kills himself.

Brutus continues to fight but becomes weary and sees that he will eventually fall. He asks several of his closest men to kill him, but they refuse. Finally he kills himself by falling on his own sword.

Antony praises Brutus, who of all the conspirators acted for what he thought was the good of Rome.

King Lear

King Lear gathers his family together and tells them he wants to divide his realm among his three daughters: Regan, Goneril, and Cordelia. He tells them he will give the largest share to the one who loves him best. Goneril and Regan flatter Lear, but Cordelia speaks her love honestly and plainly. Lear becomes angry with Cordelia. He divides his property equally between Regan and Goneril and banishes Cordelia.

Lear announces he will keep one hundred knights and his Fool to attend him, and that he will live alternately with Goneril and Regan and their husbands the Duke of Albany and the Duke of Cornwall.

The Earl of Gloucester has a legitimate son named Edgar, who is loyal to him, and a bastard son named Edmund, who is angry and resentful of his father. Edmund devises a plan to trick Gloucester into disinheriting Edgar. Edgar goes into hiding.

Lear goes to stay with Goneril. She is disrespectful and demands he reduce the number of knights attending him. Lear is outraged and leaves to live with Regan. Regan treats him in the same way.

Lear is furious. He rushes onto the heath in the middle of a storm, raging against his daughters. The Fool and a disguised Edgar accompany him. Gloucester finds them and leads them all to shelter.

Edmund betrays Gloucester to Goneril, Regan, and Cornwall, saying Gloucester was plotting with France against them. Cornwall gouges out Gloucester's eyes. Gloucester is set to wander the heath blind, and is rescued by Edgar, still in disguise.

British and French armies meet in battle and Lear and Cordelia, who has married the King of France, are captured. Edmund sends orders to have them executed.

Both Regan and Goneril have been lusting after Edmund, and he has made promises to both of them. When the intended adultery is exposed, Goneril poisons Regan, then commits suicide. Edgar returns to court and fights Edmund in a duel; Edmund is fatally wounded. Edgar reveals his true identity to his father Gloucester, who dies of shock and joy. Cordelia is assassinated and Lear slays the killer. But Lear, completely overcome with grief and recognition of what he has caused, dies.

Macbeth

Macbeth and Banquo are returning from success in battle. On the moor, they meet three witches who make strange predictions: Macbeth will be king of Scotland; Banquo will father a long line of kings, though not be king himself. Macbeth is taken with the prophecies. He tells his wife, Lady Macbeth, of his encounter and the two become consumed with ambition. The king, Duncan, is coming to stay at Macbeth's house, and Lady Macbeth convinces Macbeth to murder Duncan in his sleep. The murder takes place and Macbeth becomes the new king of Scotland. Macduff suspects Macbeth but says nothing.

However, the consequences of this brutal murder begin to weigh on Macbeth and his lady. Macbeth becomes paranoid. He fears the witches' prophecy that Banquo's sons will rule Scotland and sends assassins to kill his friend Banquo and Banquo's son. Banquo is killed but his son escapes. At a royal banquet, Banquo's ghost appears. No one but Macbeth can see it, but Macbeth begins to rage against the apparition and appears to be going mad.

Macbeth decides to visit the witches again, who make further prophecies. They warn him to beware Macduff, but also say Macbeth is safe until Birnam Wood comes against him at his castle and that no one born of woman can harm him. Macduff has fled to England, but Macbeth sends assassins to kill everyone in his castle, including his pregnant wife and young children.

Lady Macbeth's mind starts to unravel as well. She sleepwalks, wandering the corridors at night, speaking bits and pieces about the murder and trying to wash imaginary blood from her hands. Eventually she kills herself.

Macduff and other thanes decide Macbeth must be overthrown. They raise an army to come against him. The men use branches from the trees of Birnam Wood to conceal themselves as they move closer to the castle. In the heat of battle, Macbeth tells Macduff that he cannot kill him, as no man born of woman can slay him. Macduff announces he was not born of woman—he was ripped from his mother's womb through a Cesarean section. He kills Macbeth.

The Merchant of Venice

Bassanio needs a loan to travel from Venice to Belmont
to try to win the hand of Portia. He goes to Antonio, a
merchant of Venice, to ask him to lend him the money.
Antonio is a prosperous and generous Christian. He would
gladly lend the money, but all his ships and assets are at
sea. Instead, he signs a bond backing a loan from Shylock,
a Jewish moneylender. Shylock has a longstanding hatred
of the Merchant, partly because Antonio hurts Shylock's
business by lending out money at zero interest and partly
because of the religious persecution Shylock has received at
Antonio's hands. The bond Shylock gets him to agree to is
that if the Merchant does not pay back the loan by a certain
date, Shylock will cut a pound of flesh from him.

In Belmont, Portia is left a large inheritance by her
father. Suitors from all over the world come to see her. They
must listen to a riddle and try to choose correctly a gold,
silver, or lead casket. The correct box has her picture in it,
and if they choose it they will be the person she is to marry.
After several suitors choose incorrectly, Bassanio arrives and
Portia falls in love with him. She hopes he will choose the
right box, and he does. They are married. Her servant and
Bassanio's friend are also married.

Meanwhile, through a series of misfortunes, Antonio's
ships are lost at sea and he cannot deliver on the bond.
Shylock is eager to exact his justice in the court—to cut out
a pound of the Merchant's flesh, near his heart. He refuses

to take other payment on the debt, even though Bassanio, now wealthy through his marriage to Portia, has offered him twice the money owing.

At court, Portia disguises herself as a doctor of the law and makes valiant arguments for Shylock to show mercy and forgive the debt, which he will not do. He insists on following his bond to the letter of the law. He is about to proceed with taking the flesh, when she then makes the argument that if he is following the letter of the law, he can take flesh, but no blood; he can take a pound, but not an ounce more or an ounce less. After these arguments, the bond is released and the Merchant is allowed to go free. Shylock is stripped of all his money and goods. He is also stripped of his religion and told he must be a Christian.

The Merry Wives of Windsor

Sir John Falstaff plans to seduce Mistress Page and Mistress Ford. He sends them identical love letters, which they discover. They decide to lead him on in order to embarrass him. In the meantime, the women's husbands discover Falstaff's plans. Page thinks his wife will be faithful, but Ford doesn't trust his wife.

Slender, Caius, and Fenton all seek the affection of Mistress Page's daughter, Anne. Caius challenges Sir Hugh Evans (who has encouraged Slender in his suit to Anne) to a duel.

Through the help of Mistress Quickly, Mistress Ford arranges for Falstaff to visit her at her home. When Falstaff arrives, Mistress Page appears and says the angry Master Ford is on his way home. They hide Falstaff in a laundry basket; he is hauled out and dumped in the river with the laundry.

Caius and Evans have a hard time meeting up for their duel. They finally meet and prepare to fight, but end up talking between themselves. They decide they are being made fun of, one for his French accent, the other for his Welsh one.

Back at the Garter Inn, Mistress Quickly conveys a second invitation from Mistress Ford for Falstaff to visit.

Fenton speaks with Anne. She tells him her father thinks he only wants to marry her for her money. He admits that this was his original intent, but now that he has come to know her he feels differently and truly loves her.

Falstaff returns to Mistress Ford's house that night; again

Mistress Page appears and says Mistress Ford's husband is on his way home. This time Falstaff refuses to hide in the laundry basket. Instead the wives dress him in the clothes of a servant's fat aunt. When Ford arrives he mistakes Falstaff for the aunt, whom he hates. Falstaff receives a sound beating and is chased off.

Mistresses Ford and Page are happy. They think Falstaff has learned his lesson and they confess their schemes to their husbands. Master Ford promises to trust his wife and never be jealous again.

The wives and their husbands decide to publicly humiliate Falstaff. He is invited to meet Mistress Ford for a third time, this time in a haunted wood where they plan to have their children dress up as ghosts and spirits to scare him. Furthermore, Anne's parents want to use the opportunity to arrange for her elopement. Her mother wants her to run off with Caius and her father wants her to run off with Slender. Each suitor is told to wear a certain outfit so she can identify him; she is told what to wear as well. Anne, however, decides to use the opportunity to marry Fenton.

Falstaff arrives in the haunted woods. Mistress Quickly, disguised as the Fairy Queen, along with the disguised children, taunt him, pinch him, and burn him with candles. Finally the adults show themselves and the game is up. Falstaff realizes he's been played for a fool.

Slender arrives on the scene very upset. In the confusion, he eloped with a boy in Anne's outfit. Then Caius enters, also angry; he's married another boy wearing Anne's assigned clothing. Anne and Fenton enter and announce their marriage. Everyone, including Falstaff, joins in the marriage celebrations.

A Midsummer's Night Dream

Hermia's father wants her to marry Demetrius, and Demetrius wants to marry her as well. The only problem is Hermia is in love with Lysander. Hermia and Lysander decide to elope; they confide their plan in Hermia's friend Helena. However, Helena is in love with Demetrius—he used to love her, but threw her over for Hermia. Helena decides to reveal the plan to Demetrius in hopes of winning back his love. Hermia and Lysander go and hide in the woods and eventually fall asleep. They are pursued by Demetrius, who is pursued by Helena.

Meanwhile, the Duke of Athens and the Queen of the Amazon are to be married in these same woods. Oberon, king of the fairies, and his queen, Titania, have come to the forest to give their blessing to the wedding. Oberon and his queen are fighting because he wants her to give him a young Indian prince given to her by the boy's mother and she refuses. In order to get even with her, Oberon calls for the mischievous Puck to help him. He sends Puck to find a flower, the juice of which when placed on sleeping people's eyes makes them fall in love with the first living thing they see upon waking. Oberon applies the potion to the sleeping Titania. He has also seen Demetrius treat Helena badly; he decides to have Puck apply some of the flower juice to Demetrius's eyelids as well.

Soon confusion ensues. Puck mistakes Lysander for Demetrius and applies the love potion to him. When Lysander is awakened by Helena, he immediately falls in love with her, forgetting Hermia. Later Demetrius is also charmed, and he, too, falls in love with Helena.

Helena is convinced that both men are making fun of her. Hermia is enraged with Helena for stealing her lover. Lysander and Demetrius decide to duel to the death in order to prove their love for Helena, but Puck keeps them from fighting by mimicking their voices and leading them away from each other into the forest.

Meanwhile, a band of performers enters the forest to put on a play in celebration of the wedding. Bottom is the most ridiculous of the group, and Puck turns his head into that of a donkey. When the other actors see him, they run screaming into the forest. Bottom, however, is untroubled and wanders around singing. This singing awakes Titania, who sees Bottom and immediately falls in love with him. While Titania lavishes love and attention on Bottom, Oberon uses the opportunity to take the young prince.

Once Oberon has what he wanted, he enlists Puck's help to set things right. Oberon removes the spell from Titania, and Puck removes Bottom's donkey head. The spell is removed from Lysander, so he is again in love with Hermia. Demetrius is left under his spell, however, so he will remain in love with Helena. Then Puck makes all the lovers believe everything that has happened was a dream.

In the morning, the Duke and Queen arrive for their wedding. The two other couples are married along with them, and they all watch Bottom and the other performers put on the play.

Much Ado About Nothing

$\mathcal{B}$eatrice and Benedick are in love with each other. But like many lovers, they fight and quarrel, verbally sparring with each other, each trying to top the cleverness and insults of the other. They think they despise each other.

The governing men of the town decide to make a bet that they can get the two to declare their love for each other and marry. They let it be known that each harbors a secret passion for the other.

Meanwhile, Beatrice's cousin Hero is to be married to Benedick's friend Claudio. But the evil Don John decides to destroy the relationship. Hero's maid, Margaret, is in an unseemly relationship with Borachio. Don John convinces Borachio to call Margaret "Hero" at her bedchamber window at night and has Claudio spy on the encounter. Claudio is convinced that Hero is being unfaithful to him. He is devastated and seeks revenge. The next day at the altar, Claudio accuses Hero of infidelity and refuses to marry her.

The friar who was to perform the marriage believes in Hero's innocence. He devises a plan to pretend that Hero is dead, killed by the shock and shame of her rejection. This tragedy, he is convinced, will force Claudio to recognize Hero's innocence and bring the truth to light. Beatrice, Hero's father, and others agree to the plan. Beatrice enlists Benedick to help in the situation.

Meanwhile, Beatrice and Benedick have found secret letters written to each other proclaiming their love. They

112

finally acknowledge that they are in love. Claudio hears of Hero's death and admits his mistake in misjudging her. Hero's father promises another wife to Claudio, but at the wedding itself, the bride is unveiled to be Hero. Claudio learns the truth; all is forgiven. Hero and Claudio marry, and the clever and brash Benedick, who has sworn he will never marry anyone, marries the lively and passionate Beatrice.

Othello

Desdemona has secretly married the Moor Othello, a general in the Venetian army. Roderigo is hurt and angry. He is in love with Desdemona and has previously asked her father for her hand in marriage. Iago, a high-ranking soldier, is angry that Othello has passed him by for a promotion and given it to Cassio instead. Iago concocts a plan for Othello's downfall.

Iago persuades Roderigo to tell Desdemona's father about her marriage to Othello. Meanwhile, Cyprus is under attack by the Turks, and Othello is called before the senate to receive orders to prepare for war. In this public setting, Desdemona's father accuses Othello of seducing his daughter by witchcraft. Othello says he has won Desdemona's heart with his stories of war and travel. Desdemona then enters and proclaims her love for her husband; she tells her father she is loyal to Othello. The senate believes the couple, and Othello leaves for Cyprus accompanied by Desdemona and the others.

In Cyprus, they learn that the Turkish fleets have been destroyed by a storm. That night, the group from Venice celebrates. Iago convinces Roderigo to fight with Cassio, telling him Cassio is a potential lover of Desdemona. Roderigo does start a fight; Othello breaks it up and strips Cassio, who is drunk, of his rank. Iago then convinces Cassio that he can get back in Othello's good graces by using Desdemona as an intermediary.

Desdemona believes Cassio has been treated unfairly

and asks Othello to reinstate his rank. This, along with Iago's continuing insinuations, convinces Othello that Desdemona is indeed having an affair with Cassio. Iago has persuaded his wife, Emilia, to steal a handkerchief from Desdemona that Othello gave her as the first token of their love. Iago then hides the handkerchief in Cassio's lodgings.

Cassio is in a relationship with the prostitute Bianca. Iago asks him about it, where Othello can overhear. Cassio is talking about Bianca, but Othello thinks he is talking about Desdemona. He becomes enraged with jealousy and decides to kill both his wife and Cassio. He enlists Iago's help in killing them. That evening Othello asks Desdemona for her handkerchief, but she cannot produce it.

Meanwhile, Iago again convinces Roderigo to attack Cassio, persuading him that Cassio is all that stands in his way to Desdemona. A street brawl ensues, both Roderigo and Cassio are wounded, and Iago, unnoticed, manages to stab Roderigo to death before Roderigo reveals Iago's schemes. Othello hears Cassio's cries and assumes Iago has killed him.

Othello confronts Desdemona in her bedchamber. She denies again and again that anything has happened between her and Cassio and expresses her great love for Othello. Othello does not believe her and smothers her with a pillow. Emilia arrives on the scene and Othello admits what he has done. Emilia realizes what has really happened; she explains that she stole the handkerchief and exposes Iago. Iago kills Emilia. Othello attacks, but does not kill, Iago. He then pulls out a dagger and commits suicide.

Richard III

The House of York, symbolized by the white rose, and the House of Lancaster, symbolized by the red rose, have long been at civil war—the War of the Roses. Finally, there is peace under the victorious Yorks, who make King Edward IV their ruler. However, Edward's younger brother, Richard, resents Edward's power and wishes to be king. Richard decides he will use whatever means necessary, including killing anyone he needs to, in order to place himself on the throne.

Richard is a deformed hunchback. He is also intelligent, manipulative, smooth-tongued, and purely evil. He has murdered the noblewoman Lady Anne's first husband, and although she knows this, she still allows herself to be persuaded into marrying him.

After arranging for the murder of his brother Clarence, Richard places the blame for the murder on King Edward. Edward is sick and when he dies, Richard is made Lord Protector of England. He is placed in charge of the country until Edward's two young sons are old enough to rule.

Richard continues to arrest and execute the people who stand in his path—noblemen who are loyal to the princes, as well as the princes' relatives on their mother's side. With the help of his political allies, Richard finally has himself crowned King of England. He places the two young princes in the Tower of London; he then sends hired assassins to murder the boys.

Richard's bloody ascent to power has angered many of the people and noblemen of England. The Earl of Richmond (of the House of Lancaster) organizes a rebellion against Richard, and many join. They meet in France and prepare to invade England. Richard decides that to solidify his claim to the throne he must marry the young princess Elizabeth, sister to the murdered princes. He arranges for the murder of his own wife, Anne, so that he will be free to marry the young Elizabeth. However, her mother (the former Queen Elizabeth) prevents this. She stalls Richard and secretly arranges the marriage of her daughter to Richmond.

Richmond's forces invade England. The night before the battle, Richard has a nightmare in which the ghosts of all those he has murdered appear to him and tell him he will die the following day. In the Battle of Bosworth, Richard falls from his horse and runs among the battle saying, "A horse, a horse! My kingdom for a horse!" Richard kills many men, thinking each one is Richmond. Richmond and Richard finally meet; Richard is slain.

The young Elizabeth and Richmond are married, reuniting the Houses of York and Lancaster.

Romeo and Juliet

The Montagues and Capulets are sworn enemies in the city of Verona, Italy.

Romeo, the son of Lord Montague, is lovesick over a girl named Rosaline. Romeo's cousin Benvolio and friend Mercutio persuade Romeo to attend a masquerade ball at the house of the Capulets in the hopes of seeing Rosaline there. Instead Romeo meets and falls in love with Juliet, the daughter of Lord Capulet.

After the ball, Romeo steals into the Capulet courtyard and hears Juliet on her balcony vowing her love for him. Romeo makes himself known to her and the two young lovers agree to be married. With the help of Juliet's nurse and Friar Laurence, who hopes their union will heal the animosity between the houses, Romeo and Juliet are married in secret the next day.

Juliet's cousin Tybalt challenges Romeo to a duel, but now that Romeo is married to Juliet he refuses to fight him. Mercutio fights the duel on Romeo's behalf and Tybalt kills Mercutio. Grief-stricken and filled with guilt and remorse, Romeo kills Tybalt.

Romeo is exiled from Verona. He secretly spends the night with Juliet. Meanwhile, Juliet's father arranges for Juliet to marry Paris; when she refuses, he threatens to disown her.

Juliet, with the help of the friar, makes a plan. She will drink a potion that makes her appear dead for two days and then she will be placed in her family's tomb. The friar will send a note to Romeo explaining the plan so that Romeo can rejoin her when she awakens. The night before the wedding to Paris, Juliet takes the potion.

Tragically, the note to Romeo goes awry. He learns of Juliet's death and thinks it is real. He buys poison from an apothecary and goes to the Capulet tomb. Paris is there to mourn Juliet's death. The two confront each other and Romeo kills Paris. He then drinks the poison. Juliet wakes to find Romeo dead, takes his dagger, and kills herself.

The Tempest

A storm rages at sea. On a nearby island, the magician Prospero and his daughter, Miranda, watch the wreckage. Miranda asks her father to help the survivors but Prospero assures her all is well. He has caused the storm to bring the people on the ship to the island. He then tells Miranda the story of her life before they came to the island.

Twelve years earlier, Prospero was the Duke of Milan. But his brother Antonio conspired against him and took his position. Prospero and Miranda were kidnapped and left to die on a raft at sea. They survived only because a loyal friend put supplies and Prospero's books on the raft with them— the books are the source of Prospero's magic.

The other inhabitants of the island include the spirit Ariel, who was trapped in a tree by a witch named Sycorax. She died and left Ariel imprisoned. Prospero freed Ariel; in exchange Ariel is bound to serve him until Prospero releases him. Caliban also lives on the island. He is the son of Sycorax, a wild man who acts more like a beast. Prospero and Miranda helped and taught Caliban, but he tried to rape Miranda and is now enslaved to Prospero.

The survivors of the shipwreck are separated from one another. Ferdinand, the Prince of Naples, comes upon Miranda and the two fall instantly in love. Ferdinand is the only man (besides her father and Caliban) that Miranda has ever seen. Prospero wants Ferdinand and Miranda to marry, but he places obstacles between them so they have to work to earn each other's love.

On a different part of the island, the stranded Italian royal party, including Prospero's brother Antonio and Sebastian (brother to the king of Naples), are quarreling among themselves and worrying about the lost Ferdinand. Ariel arrives, invisible, and causes all but Antonio and Sebastian to fall asleep. The two men contemplate killing the others in their sleep to hasten Sebastian's rise to the throne.

Caliban, gathering firewood for Prospero, runs into Stephano (a butler) and Trinculo (a jester)—two others from the shipwrecked party. At first he is afraid of them, believing them to have fallen from the moon, but soon all three are drinking together. Caliban begins to boast that he knows how to kill Prospero. He proposes that the three of them kill Prospero, steal away Miranda, and set up Stephano as king of the island.

After testing Ferdinand and making him perform physical labor for a time, Prospero sets up a marriage ceremony of sorts between Ferdinand and Miranda. He calls upon spirits that take the shapes of the Roman and Greek gods Ceres, Juno, and Iris to celebrate the rites of marriage.

Eventually, with the help of Ariel, the three separated groups are reunited in front of Prospero. Prospero confronts his brother Antonio, but then forgives him. He pardons Caliban and releases him from his service. He vows to break his magic staff and bury his book of spells in the sea. He will return with Ferdinand and Miranda to Naples to see them married. As a final gesture, Prospero frees Ariel.

Titus Andronicus

The Roman general Titus returns from ten years at war. Only four of his twenty-five sons have survived. He has captured Tamora, Queen of the Goths, along with her three sons. He has also captured Aaron the Moor. In accordance with Roman ritual, Titus sacrifices Tamora's oldest son to the gods.

Tamora is made empress of Rome, wife to the emperor Saturninus. She takes Aaron as her lover, and together they plan her revenge on Titus. First, she successfully has two of Titus's sons framed for murdering the emperor's brother. Titus offers one of his hands to be severed in exchange for his sons' lives. His hand is cut off, but his sons are beheaded anyway. Next, Tamora has her sons rape Titus's daughter Lavinia. They brutalize and disfigure her, cutting off her hands and cutting out her tongue.

Titus's last surviving son, Lucius, is banished from Rome; he joins with the Goths to attack Rome and overthrow the wicked rulers. Aaron and Tamora have a bastard child; the nurse asks Aaron to kill the child, but Aaron kills her instead.

As the aging Titus hears of each of these deaths and atrocities, they begin to affect him harder and harder. Soon he begins to act strangely and everyone assumes he has gone mad.

However, Titus is only pretending to be insane. He uses it as a ploy to lure in Tamora. She comes to him with her sons, trying to get him to convince Lucius to cease his attacks on Rome. Titus captures Tamora's sons, kills them, and cooks them up in a pie. He feeds this pie to Tamora. He tells her what he has done, then he kills her. He then kills his own daughter Lavinia for the shame of being raped.

As if this is not enough murder and mayhem, a further killing spree ensues. The emperor kills Titus. Lucius kills the emperor. Aaron is buried alive and Tamora's corpse is thrown to beasts to be torn apart. Only then does Lucius become the new emperor of Rome.

Twelfth Night

In the kingdom of Illyria, Orsino pines away for the love of
Lady Olivia. But Lady Olivia will not allow herself to fall in
love with anyone; she is in mourning for her dead brother.

Meanwhile a storm occurs at sea; a shipwreck casts the
young Viola ashore. Viola is alone and assumes her twin
brother, Sebastian, perished at sea with the others. She
disguises herself as a man, named Cesario, and applies for
work in the house of Orsino.

Orsino is fond of Viola and makes her his page. Viola
finds herself falling in love with him, but can do very little
about it as he believes her to be a man.

As part of her duties, Viola (still disguised as the young
man Cesario) is sent by Orsino to deliver his messages of
love to Olivia. Instead of being swayed to love Orsino,
however, Olivia falls in love with the messenger—Viola.

Sir Toby Belch, Maria, Sir Andrew, and other members
of Olivia's household are sick of Malvolio, the uptight,
prudish steward, spoiling all their fun. They decide to play
a trick on him. They forge a letter from Olivia that says if
Malvolio wants to earn her love he must dress in yellow
stockings and crossed garters. He should smile constantly,
act uppity, and refuse to explain what he is doing. Malvolio
finds the letter and acts upon it. He hopes to marry Olivia,
thus promoting himself to noble rank. His behavior is so
strange that Olivia thinks he has gone insane.

Meanwhile, Sebastian has survived the shipwreck

but believes his sister Viola to be dead. He is cared for by Antonio, who is an enemy of Orsino.

Sir Andrew can see that Olivia is in love with Cesario (Viola) and challenges him to a duel. When the duel is to take place, Sebastian arrives on the scene. He looks just like the disguised Viola and Sir Toby and Sir Andrew end up fighting him. When Olivia enters, she declares her love for who she thinks is Cesario and asks him to marry her. However, she is actually addressing herself to Sebastian, who has never met her before in his life. However, Olivia is obviously wealthy and beautiful so Sebastian agrees to marry her.

Antonio has been arrested by Orsino's officers. He begs Cesario for help, thinking he is Sebastian. Cesario (Viola) says she doesn't know Antonio and he is taken away, saying that Sebastian has betrayed him. For the first time, Viola thinks Sebastian may still be alive.

Malvolio is locked up in a dark room and teased and tormented by the members of Olivia's household. Viola and Orsino arrive at Olivia's house. Olivia has just married Sebastian; when she sees Viola she thinks it is her new husband and addresses him as such. This outrages Orsino. Then Sebastian arrives. With Sebastian and Viola finally together, all is revealed. Once Orsino sees Viola is a woman, he realizes he is in love with her, not with Olivia after all.

Sir Toby and Maria have been married in secret. And finally someone remembers to release Malvolio from the dark room.

The Winter's Tale

The Sicilian King Leontes and the Bohemian King Polixenes are friends from childhood. When Polixenes comes to stay in Sicilia for a nine-month visit, Leontes decides his friend and his pregnant wife, Queen Hermione, are lovers. He becomes obsessed with jealousy and decides to have Polixenes poisoned. Camillo, the servant ordered to poison Polixenes, warns him instead and the two flee to Bohemia.

Leontes becomes even more enraged at their escape. He throws his wife in prison and publicly accuses her of carrying Polixenes' child. He then sends for word from the Oracle of Delphi to confirm his suspicions.

In prison, the queen gives birth to a little girl. Her friend Paulina brings the baby to the king, thinking that his heart will be softened when he sees his daughter. Instead, the king orders Paulina's husband, Antigonus, to take the child into a deserted place and leave her there to die. Antigonus leaves the palace with the baby. The answer then comes from Delphi that Hermione and Polixenes are innocent. Furthermore, the Oracle says King Leontes will have no heir until his daughter is found.

Mamillius, King Leontes' son, dies from the strain brought on by his father's persecution of his mother. Queen Hermione dies of a broken heart.

Hermione appears to Antigonus in a dream and tells him to name the baby Perdita. Antigonus abandons Perdita on the Bohemian coast. He is then killed by a bear. Perdita is taken in and raised by a kindly shepherd. Sixteen years pass.

The son of Polixenes, Prince Florizel, meets and falls in love with Perdita. King Polixenes doesn't want his son to have anything to do with a shepherd girl. He and Camillo attend a sheep-shearing festival in disguise to spy on Florizel and Perdita. Polixenes orders Florizel never to see Perdita again. But Camillo wants to return to Sicilia and makes a plan. He helps the young lovers disguise themselves and takes them on a ship to Italy. The shepherd travels with them.

In Sicilia, Leontes has been in mourning over the loss of his family all these years. He is overjoyed to see Prince Florizel, the son of his old friend. Florizel pretends at first to be on a diplomatic mission, sent by his father, but soon Polixenes himself arrives.

When everyone has gathered together, the shepherd tells the story of how he found the baby Perdita and raised her: King Leontes realizes she is his daughter and that the heir to his kingdom is restored. Everyone goes to Paulina's house in the country to celebrate.

At Paulina's house, a statue made in honor of Hermione has recently been completed. When King Leontes sees the statue he is shaken and upset, but then a miracle occurs: the statue comes to life and Queen Hermione is restored to her husband and lost daughter.